# Sustaining Creativity and Innovation in Organizations:
# A Tool Kit

FLEVY LASRADO, Ph.D.

Order this book online at www.trafford.com
or email orders@trafford.com

Most Trafford titles are also available at major online book retailers.

ISBN: 978-1-4907-3039-4 (sc)
ISBN: 978-1-4907-3038-7 (e)

*Trafford rev. 03/25/2014*

www.trafford.com
North America & international
toll-free: 1 888 232 4444 (USA & Canada)
fax: 812 355 4082

# ACKNOWLEDGEMENTS

Author wishes to thank
**_Emirates Identity Authority_**
for the kind support towards the publication of this book.

# PREFACE

*Organizations that use idea management systems or suggestion systems can thrive as creative or innovative amid fierce competition, technology advances, and ever-changing customer preference. Yet not all organizations use this management tool effectively. It is still a challenge for organizations to sustain their idea management systems. Managers lack the knowledge of how to build their idea management systems, and they lack the tools to assess the systems. This book proposes a solution. It helps readers to understand the five building blocks required for a sustainable idea management systems then to use the author's diagnostic tool, an assessment framework, to determine how well the system is performing in regard to each building block of the framework. By assessing the performance of each building block, you can identify areas that need improvement, moving your organization toward the true results that an idea management system actually brings.*

# CONTENTS

# CHAPTER 1

# The Idea Management System

## *Introduction*

An idea management system or employee suggestion system helps organizations to sustain their innovative and creative ability amid fierce competition, technological advances, and ever-changing customer preferences. Innovation is not about just having great ideas but making things work from small improvements. So small ideas and even focusing on prioritizing problems identified by frontline employees have real value. An entrepreneurial friend had said to me that he had succeeded making an air freshener after several attempts, and eventually the product had grabbed attention and an "Innovation Award" in the United States. Ideas, whether they are small or big, should be pursued. These small ideas have the ability to turn organizations into success stories. They can become the main source of building a competitive advantage. The idea management tool well serves this purpose of capturing employees' creative ideas.

The idea management system or tool is not new. It has been around for many years, and it is also known as a suggestion scheme or suggestion system. It will elicit suggestions from employees, classify them and dispatch them to the "experts" for evaluation. After this, the suggestion might be adopted, in which case the suggestion may well be rewarded. But even if the suggestion is rejected, the suggestion maker may still be rewarded with a token gift. "Experts" are either managers or dedicated committees who evaluate the suggestions and implement the ones that work[1]. The suggestion system became popular in many countries. Japan's well-known Toyota suggestion system, established in 1951, generated over twenty million suggestions for improving manufacturing processes over a span of forty years. The average number of suggestions submitted by each employee per year is close to fifty or one suggestion per employee per week. Tata's other well-known system is almost sixty years old. In the United Arab Emirates, the most foremost scheme is that of Dubai Aluminums (DUBAL). This organization reports that the total number of implemented and awarded ideas is 116,139 since the suggestion scheme's inception about thirty years ago. Moreover, the audited savings potential of the ideas implemented in 2010 amounted to $5.32 million, which raised the total savings achieved by the suggestion scheme over the last thirty years to more than $31.8 million.

Through these systems, employees in these organizations focused on continuous improvement. Traditionally a suggestion scheme is known to have many benefits that range from simple workplace improvements to cutting costs and even generating new revenue. Some of the commonly discussed benefits of a suggestion scheme are:

- Cultivating customer service and quality
- Refining systems, methods, and efficiency
- Cultivating safety and the work environment
- Cutting costs, reducing waste, and enhancing revenue
- Making the job easier and more productive
- Facilitating continuous improvement
- Motivating employees

The success stories of suggestion schemes are many. Several organizations around the globe report their savings as a result of their idea management or suggestion schemes. Moving forward from facilitating a continuous improvement culture, the suggestion schemes evolved to become systems that capture ideas, where employees can put their ideas forward and create win-win situations. Due to the technology advancement, these sophisticated idea management systems help spur creativity and innovation in organizations.

Management may think that getting their organizations to be creative and innovative requires articulating an ideas management system with a clear vision, giving employees rewards and perhaps providing employees training and holding companywide induction programs. Although these elements are essential, they don't guarantee the success of their systems. The success achieving result is not straightforward. They key elements of its success must be identified and understood. It requires nurturing the right practices. Performances are not identical across organizations. They should therefore be evaluated in light of their idea management system goals.

So despite of its many benefits, it is still a challenge for organizations to sustain their idea management systems. Managers lack the knowledge of how to build them, and they lack the tools to assess their systems to understand how they are benefiting the organization.

In this book, the key elements—referred to as the five building blocks for the success of the idea management system—are discussed. An assessment tool is presented. The tool helps to analyze the individual idea management system and pinpoint areas for further improvement. This tool gives a broader, more grounded view of your system and how to improve the performance of each of the building blocks. The focus of this book is to go beyond the five building blocks and help organizations assess their systems. The idea is to revive and exploit the most underutilized management tool for sustaining creativity and innovation in organizations.

## What is an idea management system or employee suggestion scheme?

An idea management system or an employee suggestion system is described as a formalized mechanism that encourages employees to contribute constructive ideas for improving the organization in which they work.[2] This is a simple explanation for a suggestion system. There are others who describe suggestion systems as:

- An untapped reservoir of effort and knowledge that could improve organizational processes and effectiveness.[3]
- A means of facilitating the process of motivating employees to think more creatively, to share those creative thoughts, and to convert creative ideas into valuable innovations.[4]

- A tool that encourages employees to think innovatively and creatively about their work and work environments and to produce ideas that will benefit the organization, for which the employee will receive recognition.[5]

## History of the idea management systems or suggestion schemes

In 1721, Yoshimune Tokugawa, the eighth Shogun, placed a box called "Meyasubako" at the entrance of the Edo Castle for written suggestions from his subjects.[6] Although this is the most basic system known, the origin of an industrialized suggestion system stretches back to the nineteenth century. In 1880, William Denny, a Scottish shipbuilder, asked his employees to offer suggestions to build ships in better ways.[7] Following this, the Kodak company became a pioneer in this endeavor with its program introduced in 1896.[8] So in the business world, the formal and structured suggestion schemes were first introduced as a modern practice nearly one hundred years ago[9].

Industry associations, such as the Employee Involvement Association (EIA), then came into existence and have contributed greatly to the increased formalization, objectivity, and professionalism of suggestion programs. Formerly the National Association of Suggestion Systems, the EIA has instituted educational, statistical, and professional development programs to raise the bar of best practices in the encouragement, evaluation, development, and implementation of ideas that add value to their organizations. IdeasUK, the United Kingdom's foremost association for the promotion of employee involvement programs, was founded in 1987. Its prime purpose being to assist organizations in both the public and private sectors, it is now an organization with more than one hundred members worldwide.

Originally, schemes were introduced for the factory shop floor employees. Particularly in recent years, they have spread to white-collar areas: to clerical departments, banks, and other commercial concerns.[10] On the other hand, in Japan, the program was well known as the Kaizan Program. While Kaizen-Oriented Suggestion Systems (KOSS) are primarily interested in generating many small improvements, Western suggestion systems encourage the pursuit of innovation.[11]

## Nature and significance of a suggestion scheme

The corporations who use the employee suggestion systems vary from small to large organizations and from private to public-sector organizations. All organizations benefit from their suggestion systems, but the real success lies on the actual effectiveness of the implemented system.

The suggestion system can be very simple with limited resources, or it can be highly sophisticated, implemented department wide or organization wide. Typically, for traditional suggestion boxes, employees were required to write their suggestions on preformatted forms and post them in designated suggestion boxes or, more recently, to file their suggestions electronically.[4] The technologically sophisticated systems are superior to the stereotypical suggestion box because they:[4]

- make it easier for employees to submit ideas that will eventually be implemented
- Provide a transparent process for evaluating the suggestions
- Generate timely feedback regarding the fate of the suggestions and any rewards they earn.

Suggestion systems can aim at different types of innovation—for example, radical or incremental. It is possible for organizations to adapt to the suggestion system depending on the environment in which they operate and strategic choices they make.[12] Suggestion schemes create a win-win situation in organizations. It does not only benefit the organization, but the employees can also reap benefits in the form of rewards.[7] Employers usually have a number of objectives in mind for suggestion schemes, some dealing with improvements in processes or employee relations and others related to hard-measure outcomes.[20]

## *The goals and functions of suggestion schemes*

The goals and functions of suggestion systems are:

- To achieve greater employee involvement that eventually leads to greater tangible benefits such as cost savings, better sales, and/or intangible benefits like higher levels of morale.[20] "Tangible" ideas can result in measurable increase in profitability. "Intangible" ideas, on the other hand, do not directly influence profitability. They usually relate to items such as working conditions, employee safety, public relations, or internal communication.[7]
- To foster creativity, to elicit untapped reservoirs of ideas, to fuel both product and process innovations, to improve workplace performance, and to increase organizational commitment and accountability among employees.[8]
- Suggestion systems are also sources of innovation. They promote the implementation of new routines and facilitate the improvement and refinement of existing routines.[14]
- Suggestion systems can create an "employee voice" through which employees can express concerns and grievances to management.[15]
- From a purely financial perspective, well-implemented suggestion systems can also significantly impact an organization's bottom line.[16]
- Suggestion systems are also believed to increase employee motivation, job satisfaction, and group interaction.[17]

## *The link to creativity and innovation*

Creativity has been defined as "the production of novel ideas that are useful and appropriate to the situation." Creativity has many synonyms, such as productive thinking, divergent thinking, originality, imagination, brainstorming, etc.[18] Creative performance is also defined as products, ideas, or procedures that satisfy two conditions:[19]

- They are novel or original, and
- They are potentially relevant for, or useful to, an organization.

Creativity in organizations is a continuous search to solve problems and create and implement new solutions for the betterment of the organization, its customers, and its members.[21] The research on creativity and innovation increased during 1990s as creativity got linked to maintaining a competitive advantage.[21] Creativity is, in essence, an individual pursuit that may or may not draw on others for inspiration and validation.[22] But creativity engagement occurs in individuals, in individuals interacting, and in group work.[23]

Innovation can be understood as a process of learning and knowledge creation through which new problems are defined and new knowledge is developed to solve them.[24] It is a process by which these ideas are captured, filtered, funded, developed, modified, clarified, and eventually commercialized and/or implemented.[25] Simply put, innovation is about the creation and implementation of a new idea in a social context with the purpose of delivering commercial benefits.[26] Innovation may be classified according to the nature of the change it brings into effect.[27] Idea generation has been studied in both the fields of creativity and innovation management.[28] Hoyrup (2010) states, "Innovation is driven by employees' resources: ideas, creativity, competence and problem-solving abilities. These innovative activities are embedded in employees' daily work activities—often in working teams—on the basis of their experience and on-the-job learning."[29] Innovation at work is mainly driven by employees' ideas and successful implementation of new programs, new product introductions, or new services and depends on a person or a team having a good idea and developing that idea beyond its initial state.[30] So, creativity fuels the innovation pipeline.[25]

Idea management more clearly underpins creativity but may also trigger innovation in organizations. However, it is important to organize the process of idea extraction to idea follow-up properly, otherwise employees will not be motivated to put their ideas forward, and many ideas will be lost. [12]

## *The process involved in the idea management system*

Typically the process of implementing an idea management system begins with employees making their suggestions individually or in teams by using an information system or manually using the suggestion forms. The team or the department in charge will then assess the suggestion through an evaluation committee. Based on the evaluation committee's feedback, the employees are then informed about the status of the suggestion. If the suggestions are selected for implementation, employees are rewarded accordingly. There are mainly three key stages in the process of suggestion system. These involve the suggestion extraction, suggestion evaluation, and suggestion implementation as depicted in the diagram below:

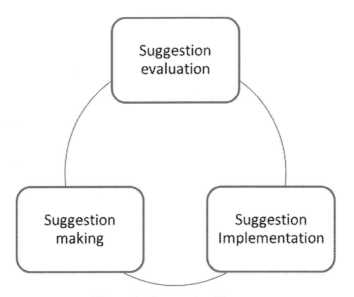

**Figure 1 : Suggestion Process**

A number of elements influence each of these stages, and therefore the right coordination and balance are required to be inbuilt into the system. These are referred to as the five building blocks of the idea management system and are discussed in the next chapters.

Suggestion making is an initial stage wherein an employee has an idea and would like to present it to the system. Using the guidelines set out by the organizations, employees prepare their suggestions. A well-formulated suggestion should be detailed enough to state how it is to be implemented and what its potential benefits are. In order to receive quality suggestions, organizations must clearly state what is considered to be an acceptable suggestion. Prior to making the formal suggestion, employees may brainstorm their ideas with colleagues, supervisors, or in teams. Organizations use paper-based, computer-based, or an online system to gather these ideas. They may design a simple form to accept the suggestions from their employees.

Once the suggestion has been received into the system, it has to be dispatched to the "experts" for evaluation. Experts are either managers or dedicated committees who evaluate the suggestions and implement the ones that work.[1] After this, the suggestion might be adopted, in which case it may well be rewarded. But even if the suggestion is rejected, the employee may still be rewarded with a token gift.

The third step is to implement the valid suggestions. Organizations may replicate them in different units if they are useful to other departments as well.

The next chapter discusses the five building blocks of the idea management system and the order of their importance.

# CHAPTER 2

# The Five Building Blocks of the Idea Management System

Implementing an idea management system is not just a matter of putting the scheme in place and rewarding the employees for beneficial suggestions. Although it begins with these, organizations need to do a lot more in order to make them fully effective and successful. Many of the challenges facing idea management systems are characteristics of traditional organizations that focus on hierarchies, rigid processes, and systems. The success of the idea management system revolves around those elements referred to as the five building blocks. These elements are not new. The key is in understanding these elements and fostering the practices associated with each of them.

The downsides of a poorly conceived ideas management system are many. They are mostly preventable. To build a successful system, it takes the five well-maintained building blocks to work together, as discussed in this book. This chapter explores these five building blocks.

The five building blocks are depicted in the picture below:

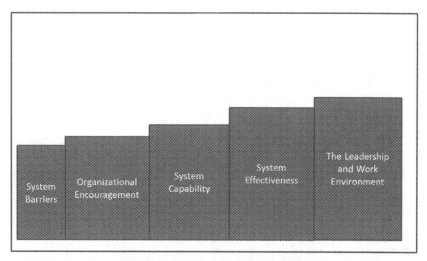

**Figure 2: The five building blocks**

These building blocks represent the core competence required for the success of the idea management system.

### Building Block 1: The Leadership and Work Environment

This factor stresses the leadership and work environment of the organization. It indicates the importance of the commitment and involvement of the top leadership and various other supportive mechanisms that must be in place to support an idea management system. The leadership and organizational encouragement indicators include:

*Top Management Support*

Top management support is a key persistent factor critical for the success of the idea management systems. It sounds simple enough, but eliciting this support isn't always as straightforward as it seems. It may appear that those in leadership positions are committed, but they really may not be absolutely committed. Because the results of the idea may not occur reasonably soon, it is possible that the top management may be tempted to reallocate resources to more lucrative projects. Top management thus needs to exhibit belief in these systems through their actions. Their responsibilities lie in making communication transparent across the organizations, emphasizing the need for creativity and innovation, and providing support and resources as required. Most importantly, the studies on various idea management systems point out that having a vision and a mission for their suggestion systems has greatly benefited organizations. The introductory briefings from the management at special events tend to exhibit the supportive nature of the top management. So support from top management is always on the list of critical success factors (CSFs) for success of the suggestion schemes. In fact, it is usually at the very top of the list. Truly, failure to get initiative means the scheme is unlikely to succeed. Employees can indeed sense when the top level support is strong or if it is weak. This may hold the employees from actively participating in making suggestions. So a visionary leadership is likely to have an impact on the success of the idea management system.

It is essential that the senior management exhibits their faith in the system and promotes it. If this happens, it encourages all managers to view it as a positive tool for continuous improvement. The higher management can help ensure that the supervisor recognizes the importance of commitment by making it one factor in his or her job performance evaluation.[31] If the senior level management support is not visible then the employees will not be motivated to turn in suggestions. It must be recognized that the employees' ideas are to be turned into either small improvements or big innovations. So, for example, while a person can be creative and generate new ideas alone, the implementation of ideas typically depends upon endorsement, backing, and resources, which essentially calls for different forms of management support. So management must get actively involved by creating the opportunities for employees to submit their ideas, get those ideas properly evaluated, give recognition when it is due, and implement them as soon as possible.

Studies have shown that a traditional, autocratic management style results in low levels of employee engagement and motivation.[32] On the other hand, leadership styles that include threats, intimidation, and coercive tactics appear to universally discourage creative behavior on the part of employees.[33] Empowering leadership has the capacity to positively influence employees' psychological empowerment, an element of importance in affecting creative outcome.[34] Therefore, the quality of leadership and management's behavior toward subordinates have an impact on employee participation.

Traditional organizations mostly emphasize on top-down approach, and it is very unlikely that they would advocate a bottom-up approach except for a few functions, such as those revolving around customer complaints. When a top-down approach is deep-rooted, employees are naturally reluctant to make suggestions, fearing job expulsions. Employees, therefore, would need the commitment and encouragement of the top management to put their ideas forward.

Top management support may be visible in many different forms. Some questions to analyze in order to understand top management support would be:

-   What evidence demonstrates top management support?
-   How can the organization describe the involvement of top management?
-   What are the supportive leadership styles that the organization is exhibiting?

Top management's commitment can thus be measured and monitored against each of the supportive factors that are relevant to the organizations. Some of the strategies that management can use to show its support of the suggestion system include:

Strategies to improve top management support:

- Establish a vision and mission for its idea management system
- Establish an "audit system" for the idea management system
- Be directly involved in programs for rewarding the best suggestions
- Directly participate in the events relating to an idea management system
- Review the system performance report quarterly/annually
- Give direction to departments that fall below the expected outcomes
- Host and sponsor events relating to creativity
- Be directly involved in making suggestions related to their own work areas, thus setting examples for their subordinates
- Exhibit support for the conferences and events relating to an idea's campaign
- Support and empower middle management

*Supervisor/Manager Support*

Supervisor support denotes the assistance of the supervisor or managers to promote the idea management system. Supervisors encourage and guide their subordinates in making suggestions. So a supervisor or a direct line manager is in fact also a key to the success of the idea management system. This is simply because they can closely support their teams in thinking and in assisting them to get their ideas down on paper. Many employees withhold good ideas when they discover that their immediate supervisors feel threatened by their idea submissions. Moreover, idea management systems used in isolation and with no close support from other managerial practices have very little chance of generating results that are profitable in the long term.[8]

Managers and supervisors have a variety of ways to influence their subordinates through goal setting and deadlines. They can adopt various leadership behaviors. Thus, the manager-employee relationship can help the creativity practice to grow in the organization. Some organizations also make the departmental heads or line managers accountable for receiving a number of ideas in order to cultivate continuous improvement in the organizations. It is also true that in organizations, managers may view the idea management system as a threat to their jobs; they may not remain loyal to such a system and hence may work against it. For this reason it is important that the line managers are taken into confidence and are given appropriate responsibilities so that they assume ownership of the system. The essential questions to address in this element are:

- What evidence is available to demonstrate supervisor support of the idea management system?
- Does the manager/supervisor have a role to play in the idea management system?

Strategies to improve supervisor support:

- Allocating responsibility to the managers for reviewing employee ideas and providing suggestions with input and assistance in refining the ideas
- Recognizing the managers for every idea from their team members
- Empowering the managers to fix the rewards for the suggestions
- Establishing some targets for managers
- Analyzing monthly and quarterly suggestion reports

*Organizational Support*

In a field where innovation is essential, most of the acute challenges do not concern innovation skills but rather the organizational context of innovation—the work communities' culture, habits, and practices.[35] So the organizational climate and cognitive-motivational-related factors such as motivation, trust, proactive, and willingness to collaborate dominate the success factors. Creativity and innovation will only be sporadic occurrences and will not thrive without a supportive environment and culture.[36] Particularly, the organization structure that establishes wrong authority often hinders tacit knowledge sharing.[37] Organizational support is any activity that facilitates employees to take part in the idea management system; that may include establishing non-rigid structures and creating a supportive organization culture.

Every organization has its own culture, which must be molded to support the suggestion system and needs to be nurtured to be beneficial in order for idea management systems to flourish. Highly successful companies like 3M and The Body Shop spend their energy and efforts on building organizational cultures and climates that perpetually create innovation. Today's workforce is very demanding and expects not only to be involved in an organization's decision-making process but also to utilize its full potential.[38] Sometimes the support rendered by coworkers motivates employees to make suggestions.

Organizational support must be analyzed by examining the various actions that an organization takes to foster the idea management system. Key questions to support this are:

- What organizational structures and cross communications exist in the organization?
- How is control exercised in an organization?
- Are there opportunities for formal and informal interaction?
- How is suggestion making facilitated?
- How would you describe the cooperation among employees within your organization?
- How does your organization motivate employees to cooperate with their colleagues?

The strategies to build this element, therefore, are:

**Organizational Support Strategies:**

- Centralized mechanisms for making suggestions
- Opportunity to replicate a suggestion elsewhere in the organization
- Empowerment to test the suggestion before submitting it into the system
- Support to review the suggestion if required
- Access to view the submitted suggestions across the organization
- Freedom to communicate with cross departments for any support
- Clear suggestion guidelines and awareness to formulate suggestions
- Creativity simulation workshops
- Facilitating collaboration
- Recognition of employees on their performance reviews

*Communication*

Creativity in an organizational transpires when information is shared with other people in the organization. So people need social and informational support to be able to create something new. It is also contended that creative ideas are more often the product of social interaction and influence than of periods of thinking in isolation.[39] Therefore a good scheme should play a role in improving communication and promoting the benefits of the idea management system. Information sharing among non-work-related individuals, who in general are not expected to possess domain-relevant knowledge, may influence creativity by facilitating remote associations and providing cognitive stimulation as well.[40] A study shows that there is a significant interrelationship between the idea providers' connectivity in the network and the quality of the innovation or ideas generated. It was found that the more-connected category performed better than the least-connected category.[28]

So related communication about the idea management system within the organization is vital. The emphasis thus has been on the need for face-to-face communication, facilitating cross-functional communication, having family and friends' support, and a free flow of information, both along the vertical axis and between units that belong to the same hierarchical level. The organization should have communication mechanisms and information sharing in the form of periodic reports on the performance of the idea management system.

In innovation literature, it is also noted that the multidisciplinary cooperative environments where firms and science and technology institutions coexist and collaborate can promote the efficiency of product development and contribute to firms' competitiveness.[41] The way in which individuals and organizations collect, disseminate, exchange, and use information influences idea generation.[42]

It is also important to provide provisions within the organization to protect employees from any obstructive behavior of colleagues as a result of their suggestions. The existence of a mechanism to deal with these issues can decrease the employees' fear for participating in the idea management system.

The questions that may be posed to analyze communication are:

- What are the communication formats that exist in the organization?
- How do you think that communication plays a role in the success of your idea management system?
- Are there any opportunities for social networking?
- What kind of information is regularly communicated?

To improve this element, some strategies that can be applied are:

Communication Strategies

- Share information in an in-house monthly newsletter
- Encourage staff to participate at national and international conferences
- Have a flexible organizational structure and non-rigid rules
- Keep an active website detailing the status of the idea management system regularly
- Have an open-door policy and open communication channels
- Increase the transparency of administrative decisions
- Have meetings and opportunities to meet with colleagues in formal and informal settings

### Building Block 2: System Capability

This factor stresses the capability of the system. The indicators to analyze the system's capability include feedback, evaluation, rewards, awareness, and system features.

*Feedback*

Feedback is concerned with how the organization disposes of the response for its employees' suggestions. Prompt and supportive feedback keeps employees motivated to make more suggestions and be involved in the system. Conveying the status of the idea to the suggestion-maker is very important because receiving no feedback can leave one feeling ignored and dissatisfied. Feedback can also help to improve the quality of the suggestion and to promptly revise the suggestion if required. Research suggests that when employees see that their suggestions are considered and applied in the workplace, they feel that they are valuable assets for the company, and they are more likely to show higher commitment. The company's lack of action on suggestions provided by non-managerial employees can demotivate them from participating in employee relation programs. Explaining the reasons for non-implementation of suggestions through appropriate communications can help to cover this issue. Employee engagement improves when job-related feedback from supervisors and managers focuses on the strengths—not the weaknesses—of employees.[43] Focusing on strengths improves employee performance, whereas focusing on weaknesses undermines the performance.

If employees do not receive feedback, they may feel that their suggestions are being ignored or that management may be taking credit for their suggestions.[44] Finally, feedback should be detailed enough to aid the personnel to know the status of their ideas, how to receive the rewards (if any), or reasons for rejection. Many suggestions will not be judged as worthy of implementation, so careful management of unfavorable feedback is essential.[4] When requested, management should provide suggestions with enough information to show that the ideas were treated impartially but should never be trapped into continually defending its decisions. To analyze and assess the feedback process, some essential questions to be addressed are:

- How do you describe the feedback system in your organization?
- Do employees receive support to resubmit the suggestions?

One of the organizations under study during this research explained that it has an online system with a complete suggestion-tracking mechanism. Employees can track the progress of their suggestions at any time. Since the supervisors are the first line of evaluators, they would get direct feedback on their suggestions. As the supervisor is also partly responsible for achieving suggestion targets, every employee is likely to get supportive and encouraging feedback. In case the employee is unhappy with the feedback, he or she still has a right to make the suggestion directly to the central system. It is also said that unsuccessful suggestions are not treated as "rejected" but shown with a status of being "not feasible at this time" to keep employees motivated. Once every fourteen days, the system will automatically remind all the users (employees, supervisors, and evaluators) if there are any suggestions pending implementation in their "in and out trays." The supervisor also has an option provided in the system to remind evaluators to enter comments for the distributed suggestions.

Interestingly, another organization had a cut-off date of fifteen days within which the feedback must be provided, and the person doing the suggesting then had a choice to appeal that decision within seven days; until and unless mutual consensus was reached, the suggestion/issue would remain active in the system.

To develop this element, some of the strategies that an organization can adopt are:

Feedback Strategies

- Informative and supportive feedback
- Reminders to evaluators and implementers about pending suggestions
- Realistic deadlines for processing the suggestions
- Provision to submit the suggestion to a central administrator if needed
- Provision for resubmissions with improvements
- Tracking systems

*Rewards*

Reward is a key element, identified as one of the success factors necessary for idea management systems. Rightly, Sweins and Jussila (2010) note that one way to give employees a piece of the action is to involve them in the financial success of the business by engaging them in a profit-sharing (PS) system. The gain-sharing program at a manufacturing unit notes that the volume of employee suggestions over time was positively related to the amount of payout received from a gain-sharing plan.[3] Further, it notes that factors that lead to the employee participation in the scheme are the size and timing of the gain-sharing bonus payout, employee perceptions of fairness regarding bonus payout, and positive, work-related, and work group communication.[3] Consistently, rewards have been recognized as one of the most important motivating factors that positively influence the success of the idea management system.

An idea management system evidently is a money saver for organizations. So employees must be rewarded not only with tangible but intangible benefits.[46] Incentives are important for employees to feel that submission of their useable ideas will be rewarded.[5] So employees should not only be recognized for their ideas, financially rewarded, and awarded with presentations in house but externally as well. The rewards should also reflect the value of the suggestion to the company. It is also crucial to note that although the rewards at American companies were a hundred times higher than those at their Japanese counterparts, American companies received only 1 percent of the number of ideas that were received by the Japanese.[12]

Du Plessis, et al. (2008) note that employees expect to be recognized or rewarded for their efforts and achievements in the organization on the basis of psychological contact with the organization. Hence, it is important that the higher-level authority in the organization ensures that they do not neglect the recognition, reward, and implementation of useable ideas and suggestions.

So depending on attention given to how participation is rewarded, organizations could improve the return on the idea capture systems. Great evidence such as lucrative reward schemes and annual rewards events was found in organizations under study. So clearly the extent to which this element is fostered in the organizations can be analyzed by asking questions such as:

- Are the employees rewarded for making the suggestions?
- Do they receive tangible or intangible benefits?
- What are the different types of tangible benefits?
- How would you explain the rewarding scheme?
- What different levels of action demonstrate the reward scheme of the organizations?
- Are the reward schemes transparent and publicized?

Some ways to improve this element in the organization are:

> Rewards Strategies
>
> - Establish financial and nonfinancial rewards
> - Establish reward categories
> - Give encouragement for taking part in local, regional, and international suggestion contests
> - Make the reward scheme transparent within the organization
> - Implement fair calculation and allocation of rewards in proportion to the savings wherever possible

*Awareness*

The awareness indicator explains the publicity that the organization takes with regard to its idea management system. It is important that everyone in the organization is aware of the benefits gained from implemented suggestions so that they, too, may be encouraged to think about the ways in which they can contribute. The idea management system must be publicized at launch and at regular intervals throughout the year in order to ensure that everyone is aware of its existence. The most common problems that organizations encounter with idea management systems are too few useable suggestions or finding that running a scheme is too expensive or timeconsuming.[47] Therefore, one of the ways to overcome these challenges is to raise the profile of the scheme by publicizing it in new employee induction packs, at various events, or by setting various ideas campaigns throughout the organization periodically. Moreover, if ideas are made public, these ideas, good and bad, could have started other creative ideas elsewhere in the organization.[48] There must be constant, subtle "marketing" tied in with periodic contests or other splashes of recognition if employee interest is to be maintained. An organization under study during this project explained that it conducts awareness campaigns and has given a name to its scheme, "Have Your Say," to attract more suggestions from employees. Another organization that had been using the idea management system for about thirty years holds promotional events such as annual celebrations for the system, and it has of minimum two pages of update in monthly newsletters about the system. The organization recalls that when it had put up a promotional campaign for five days, it received about six thousand suggestions. Some others also support having thematic campaigns. To assess and analyze this element, some of the questions to address are:

- Is there a formal awareness program, such as notice boards, induction, website, etc?
- Are there specific events taking place to highlight the idea management system?
- Does the in-house (or any) newsletter report the success stories of the idea management system?

Some of the strategies to improve awareness include:

**Awareness Strategies**

- Hold promotional events.
- Set up newsletters, websites, banners, and notice boards.
- Hold thematic campaigns monthly.
- Have an employee induction program.
- Establish a brand name for the suggestion scheme.

*Evaluation*

To choose the ideas for implementation, there must be appropriate criteria; if not, innovation will suffer.[49] Therefore, the biggest obstacles in the suggestion cycle lie in the area of review, evaluation, and guidance.[50] Whether the system uses full-time evaluators or department personnel, the evaluation process needs to be specified in detail since it forms the heart of the idea system.[51] When the review and evaluation and guidance aspect of the system functions properly, it can be a great motivating force that will attract many excellent proposals.[50]

A cautious thought should be given to the evaluation strategy. Those who are given responsibility for evaluating suggestions must be fully committed to the success of the scheme. A quick evaluation and realization of suggested ideas motivate employees and contribute to the improvement of the innovative capacity of the organization.[42] Establishing a standing committee for evaluation of employee suggestions, therefore, is recommended. An organization that was studied during this research explained that its evaluation team consists of a system chairman, system superintendent, twenty-eight area representatives, and three advisors representing engineering, finance, and safety departments. Such diverse teams can evaluate the suggestions effectively and promptly. An evaluation construct that includes elements such as novelty, originality, paradigm relatedness, workability, acceptability, implementability, relevance, applicability, effectiveness, specificity, completeness, and implicational explicitness of an evaluated idea would be more beneficial as well.[21] So to analyze the evaluation element, it is therefore necessary to understand:

- How an evaluation committee is established
- If there are set procedures and transparent processes to evaluate the suggestions
- If the reasons for rejected suggestions are communicated

Strategies to Improve the Evaluation

- Dedicated schedule to evaluate the suggestions
- Dedicated evaluation team
- Providing reasons for rejected suggestions
- Making the evaluation procedures and team members transparent
- Having evaluation criteria

*System Features*

To handle employee creativity effectively, it is important to have a simple, formal, and effective system. A mechanism through which employees can make their suggestions is necessary to elicit employee ideas. The main benefits of such schemes first of all enhance the number and the quality of ideas.[42] Therefore, the development of an arrangement with simple procedures for submitting suggestions is a key aspect of the idea management system.

The guidelines to submit suggestions are important. This is to elaborate which topics are open to suggestions. These will likely include ideas that affect cost savings, quality, productivity, process improvements, workplace safety, revenue generation, morale enhancement, etc. Otherwise, employees are likely to use it as a complaint box or raise concerns relating HR matters. The guidelines must also elaborate that it is not just a mere suggestion but should outline the procedure for implementation. Indeed it is easy to flash an idea, but realization requires some details to understand if it is worth implementation. Therefore, these details should be known to the employees to avoid the "garbage in, garbage out" phenomena. An illustration of "why" and "how" the idea will impact the organization should be of benefit. However, caution must be taken not to make the suggestion-writing process too tedious, such as employees having to fill in multiple pages of suggestion forms.

An idea management system designed with usability in mind will improve innovation among employees and hence increase participation.[6] The best way to kill a system is to let an idea remain in the process for days or months. The goal should be to completely process a suggestion in about fifteen days and in no more than sixty days. Therefore, idea management systems must be expertly administered, and the ideas gathered must be quickly and swiftly processed.

The system should be clear, easy to use, and must have fair and consistent policies. Simple and effective systems encourage employees to make more suggestions when compared to the less attractive ones.[6] The electronic systems are more useful than the suggestion box because they make it easier for employees to submit ideas, provide a transparent process for evaluating the suggestions, and generate timely feedback regarding the status of the suggestions and any rewards they earn. Such a system can help to monitor the progress of the scheme on a regular basis. The more comfortable employees are with the format, the more suggestions will be received and the more money will be saved.[44] Finally, having a system that makes it easy for employees to contribute ideas increases the likelihood that good ideas will be submitted.[52]

Employees get frustrated when they see their ideas being ignored for a long time. It is important, therefore, to process the ideas submitted into the system regularly, for which an effective administration system is necessary. An expert administration would largely motivate employees to be involved in the system. Moreover, the ideas are to be received from every realm of the organization irrespective of their role and position. Employees often may not possess the skills necessary to put forward their suggestions; the dedicated and skilled administrators would guide employees in formalizing their suggestions. Such help would encourage employees to put their ideas forward without any hesitation. The manual idea management systems fail because of their poor administration. An effective idea management system can help to overcome these obstacles, and is hence a critical success factor that can effectively contribute to its sustainability.

The system features can analyzed by finding answers to:

o   What is the process followed to elicit employee ideas?
o   Are there any guidelines to make a suggestion?
o   Is there any help available if required?
o   How would a person making a suggestion know the status of the suggestion (if it is filed in the system or not)?

Clearly, some of the strategies to improve this element would include:

Strategies for Improving the System Features Element

- Dedicated idea management system administrator
- An electronic system to receive and timely process the suggestion
- Established roles and responsibilities to all stakeholders with regard to idea management systems
- Multiple ways to submit suggestions

*Resources*

This indicates the extent to which the organization supports its employees with resources needed for developing ideas and honoring the employees. Adequate and timely availability of the resources can increase the sustainability of the idea management system. One of the main influences for a successful implementation is the resources allocated.[50]

An adequate budget must be provided to fund awards or other forms of recognition, the purchase of equipment, and promotion and publicity of the scheme.[54] The committed resources are required at three stages of idea management systems, i.e., idea generation, idea landing, and idea follow-up.[12] When these requirements are met, a transfer will take place from employee creativity to practicable ideas, giving organizations a large and constant supply of relevant project ideas.

The success of the idea management system lies not only in generating the creative ideas but also in the implementation of these ideas. Indeed resources support the idea realization process. If organizations lack the necessary resources, even the best suggestions received won't be fruitful. The diminishing work engagement of employees can be improved if the employees receive adequate resources.[43] So an approved budget to support the administrative resource, promotional activity, and the cost of the awards or technical resources can boost creative performance. In addition, there must be some established way of availing physical resources to test their ideas. Resource support can be assessed through the following:

- Is there availability of financial resources to support the idea management system?
- Is there a procedure to seek resources?
- Are employees allowed to escalate any related matters to their superiors and superiors, in turn taking it to higher management for a swift action?

Some of the strategies to foster resource support are:

> • Make budgetary provisions to support employee creativity
> • Allocate resources if required

## Building Block 3: System Effectiveness—The Critical Success Criteria

This factor emphasizes the benefits of the idea management system. These are the essential outcomes of the suggestion system. Hence it can be termed critical success criteria. It is essential here to differentiate the critical success factors and the critical success criteria. The critical success criteria can be seen as result areas of the suggestion schemes that the organization achieves.[54] The critical success criteria mainly represent the outcome of the suggestion scheme and can be described broadly as system benefits. The critical success factors are those levers that the organization can pull to increase the effectiveness of the suggestion scheme.[54] Gupta, et al (2005) explain that sustaining quality programs have direct impact on improved business process, improved quality service, and improved customer satisfaction. The improved processes and services can lead to new revenue generation and cost savings.

The indicators for the system's effectiveness include:

- Customer satisfaction: The purpose of the idea management system is to improve customer satisfaction. An improvement in customer satisfaction increases the sustainability of an idea management system.
- Product quality: One of the stated goals of the idea management system is to improve the quality of the product or service. An improvement in product quality or service as a result of this system increases the sustainability of the system itself.
- Improvement process: The other objective of the idea management system is to continuously improve the organization's processes. Meeting this objective of the idea management system increases the system's sustainability.

- Employee productivity: This indicator implies the benefit that the organization gains in terms of employee productivity. Idea management systems help improve employee safety and satisfaction, resulting in employee productivity. Idea management systems also improve employee commitment and sense of accountability to the organization, resulting in employee productivity. The other stated benefits of the system are that it helps employees to perceive a sense of security and to improve employee confidence in the organization.
- Profitability: Indicators imply the costs saved or new revenue generated as a result of an idea management system.

Customer satisfaction is the priority in all organizations that were under study. They, therefore, extend their systems to include customer input as well. Product improvement and product quality are also the desired outcomes in these organizations; this was assessed based on the number of processes that are improved due to the suggestions of employees and how the products or services have been enhanced from their initial launches. Organizations loudly announced their savings on their web portals, and there is evidence of small amounts to larger amounts. To assess and analyze the outcomes, a number of key questions to be addressed are:

- Are suggestions in relation to workplace improvements and safety encouraged?
- Are there any provisions for customers to suggest improvements?
- Is continuous process improvement a culture in the organization?
- Is there any evidence of quality enhancements?
- Are there financial benefits to the organization?

Some of the ways to foster this element are:

- Adopt and replicate the work improvement suggestions.
- Focus on service and product quality improvements.
- Create success stories of cost savings or new revenues.
- Assess the customer satisfaction rates regularly.

## Building Block 4: Organizational Encouragement

This factor stresses the supportive elements that exist within the organization to support the idea management system. The indicators of this block are teamwork, employee participation, and training

*Teamwork*

Teamwork implies a possibility for employees to collaborate and make joint suggestions. Awards in this case would be given to the entire team. Employees can team up with colleagues from other departments as well. Providing an opportunity to make suggestions in groups can drive out the employees' fears of losing face if the suggestion is not accepted. Interestingly, it is claimed that the benefits of a modern, well-managed idea management system lie not in the immediate financial returns but in the contribution made to achieving greater involvement and teamwork.[56] If suggestions are encouraged from groups, employees are more likely to generate creative ideas.[57] Anonymity positively affects the groups' performance in idea generation, reducing the evaluation effect, and the fear of disagreeing. An organization even illustrated that when the suggestions come from teams, they generally have a higher value. However, it must not be that all suggestions are accepted in groups as there is evidence that in some organizations individuals tend to make more suggestions than in groups since they are not open to ideas of sharing the benefits.

Some of the strategies to improve the performance of the system in relation to teamwork are:

Teamwork Strategies:

- Provision to submit ideas in teams
- Team rewards

*Training*

This implies the extent to which an organization provides training to stimulate the creativity of employees and their ability to use the idea management system effectively. It is generally found in the organizations that send individuals to seminars, training programs, and conferences as a reward for their creativity, increasing their commitment to the scheme. It was predicted that trained groups and individuals will generate more ideas in subsequent brainstorming sessions than untrained groups and individuals and that the effects of training will be more beneficial for interactive groups than nominal groups.[58] It is observable that firms invest in training their employees to increase organizational competitiveness, profitability, and to boost employee morale and behaviors.

> Strategies to Influence Training
>
> • Creativity-related workshops and training
> • Training to use idea management systems
> • Guidelines or user manuals to use the idea management system

*Employee Participation*

This implies the extent to which employees participate in the idea management system. Greater involvement of employees improves the sustainability of the idea management system.

It is true that good ideas can come from anyone, at any level, anyplace, and anytime.[59] Therefore, every member of the staff should be encouraged to participate in the scheme.[47] Employee participation is the foundation of the idea management system.[60] Therefore, employees need to be motivated and encouraged for their involvement. One of the biggest reasons employees do not pass their ideas up the line is that no one asks them. The level of employee participation in decision making is a strong indicator of willingness to engage in behavior that supports the organization. The employees' domain knowledge and expertise increase the ability to make suggestions. Expertise is a substantial factor in creativity. Employees who have the information, power, and skill needed to make decisions on a wide range of issues are therefore more creative.

So the other crucial element for the success of the idea management system is employee participation. Furthermore, they don't particularly focus on suggestions that are meant only for cost saving. Suggestions can involve any improvement, such as improvement in employee morale or job satisfaction. Organizations display the status of participation rate yearly. Some organizations link the suggestion making to their performance review or set dedicated targets, while others leave it as optional participation. At the same time, making participation in an idea management system mandatory for employees and creating an environment of competition often has a negative impact on the idea management system. A free and voluntary environment will positively impact the idea campaign.

Some of the strategies to influence participation are:

- Making the scheme open to all employees
- Setting participation targets (minimum suggestions per year)
- Encouraging suggestions for any area and not necessarily for cost savings
- Having no strict boundary between job roles and creativity

## Building Block 5: System Barriers

This factor implies the existence of unsupportive practices that hinder the idea management system. These barriers have a negative impact on the system and include job control and creating a sense of competition among employees.

### Job Factors

A job factor implies the extent to which employees are expected to follow the standard routines within their job roles. Jobs with tight time pressures and standard routines impact the creative ability of employees and discourage them from participating in the idea management system. Employees who have more autonomous and broader roles and who are more confident in performing activities outside the technical core of their work are most likely to make suggestions.[61] Individuals are more creative when they are interested in the task itself and enjoy the process of working on the task and when they feel motivated primarily by the interest, enjoyment, satisfaction, and challenge of the work itself.[39] So as long as employees experience a higher quality of work life, their creativity will also remain high. Some of the barriers for creativity stated by Wong, et al (2003) are:

- Low commitment to organization and system
- Fear of change and criticism
- Time and work pressure
- Rigid rules and company style

Sadi and Al-Dubaisi (2008) evaluated the factors that prevented the creativity of marketing executives in Saudi Arabia. Their study focused on the evaluation of six factors believed to be the barriers to creativity. They noted self-confidence and task achievement as the most significant barriers to creativity. The management practice demands that task completion has a top priority and does not leave much room for creative thinking. Organization structures have to be modified in different industries so that the organizational structure of a company or a department supports transfer and transmission of tacit knowledge in the best way. The organization structure often hinders tacit knowledge sharing by establishing wrong authorities. Further, unclear goals and unclear incentives can inhibit tacit knowledge transfer for fear of losing ownership, a position of privilege, or superiority, having a lack of sufficient rewards, or even sometimes due to being unaware of the fact that their knowledge might be of interest to others, as well as difficult relationships between sender and receiver and absorptive capacity, which happens if the receiver is not able to deal with the ambiguity of the system, and therefore the probability of failure increases.

Organizations demonstrate that the flexible and supportive work environment, innovation supportive practices, and freedom to try new things boost the performance of idea management systems.

The strategies below can improve the performance of the system:

Strategies for Job Factor Element

- Creating a flexible work environment
- Establishing job autonomy or ownership of tasks
- Supportive culture to take risks and try new things
- Opportunity to meet or share ideas across the organization

Although the factors are discussed independently, they relate to each other and have impact on each other. At this stage it is important to understand their order or importance levels. In the next section, the importance level of each of these building blocks is discussed.

**The Level of Importance of the Five Building Blocks**

While all of the five building blocks are necessary for the success of the idea management system, it is also vital to note the importance of each of them. They are interrelated and build on each other. The importance of the five building blocks can be depicted as in figure 3 below.

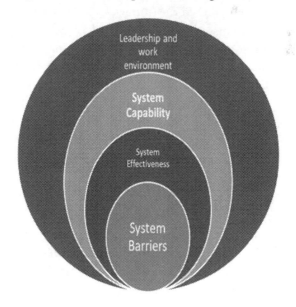

The most important factor is placed at the top layer, and it is the leadership and work environment. Leadership and work environment matter largely because they are the essential support to foster any of the other supportive elements such as rewards, training, resources, flat organizational structures, environments, and teamwork; making the scheme open to all requires top management backing. Many of the vital elements can only be nurtured upon obtaining this go-ahead from the top management. This indeed has implications for management. First, to have vision and outline the mission and goals for the system, and also recognizing employee participation in the decision-making process, which is vital for the success of the business in a society where a knowledge-based workforce is gaining importance.

The second important factor is the system capability placed in the second layer. Truly, a mechanism will then have to play a role to elicit creative ideas. It must be robust and have the essential features to motivate employees to use a scheme effectively and efficiently. Without such a backbone support, employees will not bother to make suggestions. It calls for formal recognition of employees' ideas and establishing the ground rules for the appropriate functioning of the system.

The third important factor is system effectiveness. When the top two elements are synchronized then the third element focuses on the outcomes. Setting up an idea management system and having no tangible benefits would only add to the further difficulties of the organization. It is essential that it at least achieves the desired goals and outcomes effectively.

The fourth factor is organizational encouragement. The additional supportive elements play a role when an initiative is launched, and its performance requires that the levels of effectiveness are stretched for maximum impact. These elements can only play a role when the preceding factors are established.

The fifth important factor is improving system barriers. Finally, focusing only on the levels would not lead to success. There must also be an approach to eliminate the factors that hinder performance. This factor complements organizational encouragement and mostly attempts to avoid the organizational impediments that would impact the system negatively.

# CHAPTER 3

## Sustainability and Its Stages

The meaning of "sustainability" implies the ability to sustain and maintain a process or object at a desirable level of utility.[64] Simply put, the sustainability of something means persistence regarding the time of the thing—for example, if a building is left without maintenance, the aging of materials and environmental factors will make the building enter a state where it cannot sustain itself and will collapse.[65] So the term "sustainability" implies the ability to continue in an unchanged manner.[66]

Zairi and Liburd (2001, p. 452) define sustainability as "the ability of an organization to adapt to change in the business environment to capture contemporary best practice methods and to achieve and maintain superior competitive performance."

For an industry to become more sustainable, the responsibility of its activities should be expanded from the production site to the whole product chain.[68] Idris and Zairi (2006) explain that Total Quality Management (TQM) sustainability could be viewed from the effectiveness of TQM implementation that is based on prescriptive critical factors and effectiveness of critical factors that generate sustainable excellence. Similarly, sustaining innovation within organizations involves several coordination challenges that center on how ideas can be translated across space and time.[70] The continuous improvement of industrial activities with respect to product sustainability also implies cost and time efficiency, product and process quality.[71] Similarly, Presley and Meade (2010) explain sustainability in the construction industry as being more profitable and more competitive, delivering buildings and structures that provide greater satisfaction, giving a feeling of wellbeing and value to customers and users, respecting and treating its stakeholders more fairly, enhancing and better protecting the natural environment and minimizing its impact on the consumption of energy, reducing waste, and avoiding pollution during the construction process. Thus, the concept of sustainability applies to all aspects of functional and operational requirements.[64]

## Sustainability of Idea Management Systems

It is necessary to define the sustainability of a suggestion system to avoid it being perceived diversely. Rapp and Eklund (2007), for example, studied the suggestion schemes that were operational for longer periods of time and derived the enablers that helped to keep the program alive over a period of time. Although the longevity is one dimension, sustainability of a suggestion system needs to consider the achievement of the stated stakeholder goals. Some studies evaluate the effectiveness of their schemes in terms of number of suggestions received and the number of suggestions implemented, but the sustainability assessment is not disclosed in only these parameters because it needs to be assessed through its key success factors. Suggestion schemes are designed to achieve a number of goals for the organizations. Organizations should have stated goals for their suggestion scheme, and the success of the suggestion scheme, therefore, should be assessed against achievement of these stated goals. Thus, sustainability of a suggestion system should be positioned to ensure that it:

- Adds value to the organization through tangible or intangible benefits
- Creates a conducive work environment for improved productivity
- Ensures employee wellbeing and increases employee job satisfaction
- Improves employee morale and thus continues to keep its employees involved in the suggestion schemes
- Improves employees' confidence and builds a sense of security among its employees
- Improves work process or service
- Improves customer satisfaction

When assessing industry sustainability, generally the indicator-based frameworks that address all three dimensions of sustainability—environmental, social, and economic indicators—are used.[73] Indicator-based frameworks have a wide focus as they can incorporate different dimensions.

So the expectations from the system must be set in the language of those involved and should measure things on which they can have direct impact.[74] The TQM practices are evaluated by using parameters such as balance sheets, bottom lines, market shares, revenues, and shareholder values. The dilemma is that the sustainability of TQM practices is not disclosed in these parameters.[75] Similarly, the mere outcomes, such as quantity of suggestions received, quantity of suggestions implemented, or just an increase in the bottom line only, cannot be considered as parameters to disclose sustainability.

This perspective firstly hints that sustainability should first consider the performance perspective. Second, sustainability should also imply meeting the stated objectives of the initiative, and it is not just a binary state of sustaining or not sustaining. Rather, it is influenced by a number of factors. Similarly, to assess the sustainability of a suggestion scheme, the key elements that focus on these perspectives need to be considered.

The sustainability of a suggestion scheme, therefore, can be defined as "the achievement of stakeholders' stated goals involving competence management, profitability, employee productivity, and continuous process improvement now and in the future."

### Stages in Sustainability

The practices associated with an indicator range from its lowest form to a higher level. These practices, as discussed earlier, can be improved or developed beyond the initial stage to the advanced stage. Thus, the sustainability of a suggestion system in a particular organization can be understood as at its initiate stage, at its developmental stage, or at an advance stage, as depicted in the figure below.

The initial stage is conceptualized as a beginning stage where there is little or often an absence of practices relating to the factor indicators. It is also possible that some adverse practices are present, negating the impact of an indicator at this stage. The developmental stage could be conceptualized as exhibiting adequate evidence for each of the indicators. A good set of practices for each of the indicators implies an advanced status. At this stage, each of these indicators can demonstrate good evidence of the practices relating to each of the indicators.

The section below explains the practices associated with each of the stages, i.e., initial, developmental, and advanced.

## Leadership and Work Environment

A suggestion system exhibits robust evidence for the top management's support in established organizations. The commitment and involvement are exhibited in a number of formats. However, at the initial stage, this commitment and form of support are not very visible but are gradually developed. On the other hand, there might be some adverse actions that can hinder the success of the suggestion system—for example, a suggestion system is implemented in isolation, and employees are not at all motivated to participate.

Supervisor support is crucial for the success of the suggestion system. Supervisors' guidance and encouragement are the basic requirements for the success of the suggestion scheme. To develop this support, it is then necessary that organizations formalize this facilitation by making the supervisors responsible for the success of the suggestion system, and this could be further moved to its advanced level by empowering and also recognizing them on awarded suggestions. At the same time, supervisor support could be undermined if the organization does not recognize the role of the supervisor in the success of the suggestion system.

At an initial stage, organizations provide guidance on types of suggestions and how to make them. They develop centralized or decentralized systems to review the ideas. Organizations move beyond their initial stage to the developmental stage to create a supportive organization culture. At an advanced level, they organize creativity simulation workshops and options to replicate the ideas across the organization and develop central repositories. Organizations can hinder the creative ability of employees, and success of the suggestion system may be put in danger if the organization's basic culture is not innovation-supportive. For example, rigid rules and organizational structure fostering a pressurized work environment can have negative impacts.

Organizations encourage open communication and provide opportunities to meet and share ideas through formal or informal meetings. This facilitation is further developed by strengthening communication through usage of in-house newsletters or websites and avoiding the barriers for communication among departments. Organizations can further create opportunities for networking with external and internal parties for sharing ideas and stimulating creativity.

Employees need to be protected from coworkers' disruptive behavior. Organizations provide support to resolve disputes arising as a result of suggestions. If employees are to sort out the disputes on their own, it would have a negative impact on the suggestion system.

Organizations demonstrate that the comfort and guidance of workers motivate them to make suggestions. But, of course, such support is visible in organizations that demonstrate a long standing of the suggestion system and where advanced facilities, such as options to submit suggestions for colleagues, are given. The practices that instill negative impacts here are when employees hinder the success by simply not supporting a colleague's initiative.

System Capability

The success of the suggestion system depends on evaluating and implementing valid suggestions. Organizations should demonstrate that they implement suggestions. The implementation rate should gradually improve. The advanced organizations further ensure that they award only implemented suggestions. The performance status report is shared among all stakeholders. Organizations may sometimes invite ideas and not implement them at all. Managers take the ideas of their subordinates and act as if they are their own, giving a feeling of taking a free ride.

It is necessary that employees be given job autonomy to exhibit their creativity abilities. Organizations further demonstrate that they value their employees and encourage participation by giving them an opportunity to take part in decision making. Tight work routines and pressurized work environments hinder creativity greatly.

Feedback is one of the most important components of the suggestion systems. Organizations therefore set deadlines for processing the suggestions. It is not sufficient to only process the suggestions within the deadlines, but feedback needs to be supportive and cooperative. Organizations therefore ensure that the system is organized to make sure that encouraging feedback is given. On the other hand, organizations may provide discouraging feedback and demotivate employees.

Rewards are key components of suggestion schemes. Organizations therefore set up financial benefits or some recognition mechanism. Organizations at a developmental stage ensure that there is a transparent process of rewards and recognition. At an established state, the rewards are also calculated in proportion to the value of the suggestions.

At an initial stage, it is necessary that an effective evaluation process is in place to assess the suggestions. Organizations depending only on teams or managers to validate the ideas may have an adverse impact. Evaluation could be developed by making this process transparent to employees or creating more awareness of the evaluation process; upon completion of the evaluation process, employees should give a fair chance to appeal if needed.

Organizations create awareness of their schemes using common communication mechanisms. At a developmental stage, the campaigns are more focused and use advanced mechanisms for promotion.

Organizations will have a system to receive employees' ideas and process them on time. This is improved by implementing electronic and user-friendly systems. Established organizations then install dedicated administrators and central systems and develop clear roles and responsibilities.

Organizations set side financial resources to support the suggestion system. They build mechanisms to distribute resource support to stimulate employee creativity.

System Effectiveness

Customer satisfaction is evident in the established schemes; if there is no evidence of this benefit, the scheme is at initial stage. The improvement in processes is evidenced in the established schemes; if there is no evidence of this benefit, the scheme is at an initial stage. Moreover, the objective of the scheme would be to elicit suggestions for improving the processes.

The established suggestion systems exhibit good savings as a result of suggestion scheme. If there is no evidence of this benefit, the scheme is at initial stage. In an established scheme, suggestions aimed at employee morale and resulting in employee productivity would be rewarded with an appropriate reward scheme. Employees would feel safe in and satisfied with their jobs. Their confidence in their organizations would be improved. Thus, this would result in their making more suggestions.

For the success of the suggestion systems, it is necessary that there are no barriers to creativity, and as such employees are free to carry out their tasks and employees don't work under pressure at all times. The greater such support from organizations is on these parameters, the better the result of the suggestion system.

Organizational Encouragement

Teamwork is encouraged and team rewards are offered in established schemes. Employee domain knowledge and experience is also instrumental in the success of the suggestion system. Organizations demonstrate that due to their talented employees, their systems are successful. They also note that, over periods, it is skilled employees who make more suggestions and established schemes attract rewards at local or international levels.

Organizations support their employees through training relating to suggestion system usage, but the established organizations further establish creativity-stimulating training, whereas training is not very common initially.

Established schemes ensure that they receive suggestions relating to any improvement and not necessarily relating to saving costs. Established schemes also demonstrate that they participate at local and international competitions, and, moreover, they do not draw a strict line between the job description and creativity. At a developmental level, schemes would be made open to all, and the status of employee participation is made public. Organizations also limit participation to certain employees, and this would keep the sustainability of a suggestion system low.

System Barriers

Competition is a major barrier for the success of the suggestion system. The existence of such a practice brings the sustainability of a suggestion system very low. Established organizations therefore ensure that employees participate at their own will and make it clear to their employees that they are not judged by their performance. This may not be well stated at initial stages.

In summary, the practices associated with each of these stages are outlined below.

1. The key practices that are associated with the initial stage are:

   ✓ A little visibility of the top management's involvement in suggestion system activities
   ✓ Supervisors provide guidance and encouragement to submit ideas but are not directly responsible or not made accountable for the success of the suggestion system.
   ✓ Clear suggestion guidelines and awareness to formulate suggestions are available.
   ✓ Little evidence of open communication within the organization (e.g., formal or informal meetings) and minimum opportunity for networking internally and externally
   ✓ No evidence or support to control the disruptive behavior of coworkers

✓ Employee collaboration and support for each other is not very visible.

✓ Minimum type of financial rewards, and they are not linked to the value of the suggestions

✓ There is feedback to the employees on their suggestions.

✓ There is a dedicated schedule to evaluate the suggestions, a dedicated evaluation team, and evaluation criteria.

✓ There is a system to elicit the employee's creative ideas.

✓ The cost savings or new revenues are minimal.

✓ There is little improvement in employees' sense of accountability and commitment to their organization, employees' job satisfaction, or employees' confidence in an organization.

✓ No evidence of customer satisfaction or product quality improvement as a result of suggestion systems

✓ Employee participation is limited to few employees.

✓ Organization has limited talented employees.

✓ Employees have standard work routines and mostly work under pressure.

✓ Employees feel pressured to make suggestions as they believe that they are judged on their performance through the suggestion system.

2. The key practices for the developmental stage include:

✓ Top management has established a vision, mission, and robust policies and procedures for the smooth functioning of the suggestion scheme.

✓ Supervisors are made responsible for suggestion schemes by setting up targets.

✓ There is good evidence of open communication within the organization.

✓ There is a provision to dissolve any disputes among employees, and employees collaborate to make suggestions.

✓ A reward scheme is transparent, and there is usually an improvement in the rate of suggestion implementations.

✓ It has a provision to replicate an implemented solution elsewhere in the organization, and the organization often creates success stories.

- ✓ Provides encouraging feedback to the employees on their suggestions
- ✓ The evaluation procedures and names of evaluation teams are transparent.
- ✓ There is a user-friendly and electronic system to receive and timely process the suggestions.
- ✓ Adequate resources are available, and there is a procedure to avail physical resources as required to support creativity.
- ✓ A moderate amount of new revenue generation or cost savings is evidenced.
- ✓ Adequate evidence of improvement in employees' sense of accountability and commitment to their organizations, job satisfaction, and in employees' confidence in an organization
- ✓ There is adequate evidence of process improvements taking place, and there is evidence of customer satisfaction as a result of suggestions.
- ✓ Team suggestions are encouraged; creativity-related training is provided.
- ✓ Moderate flexibility in working environment, usually no standard work routines, and employees don't work under pressure
- ✓ Employees are somewhat informed that participation is not mandatory but is tied indirectly to its success through different target settings

3. The key practices for the advanced stage include:

- ✓ Top management is directly involved in suggestion making and suggestion system-related activities.
- ✓ Supervisors guide their subordinates and are empowered to make decisions.
- ✓ Creativity stimulation workshops are often facilitated.
- ✓ Constant flow of information through websites, newsletters, etc., and employees can submit suggestions for their colleagues
- ✓ Rewards are fairly calculated as per their savings and have numerous special annual award categories.
- ✓ Provision to submit the suggestion to central administrator if needed and a chance to appeal the decision at least once
- ✓ Provide reasons for rejected suggestions

✓ A dedicated suggestion scheme administrator to monitor the system is available; the roles and responsibilities for all the stakeholders are well stated.

✓ There is good evidence of new revenue generation or cost savings.

✓ Suggestions are encouraged for any area and not necessarily for cost savings

✓ No strict boundary between job role and creativity

✓ Suggestions get awarded at local or international competitions.

✓ No standard work routines or work pressures

✓ Employees are well informed that they participate in a suggestion scheme at their own will and that they are not judged for their performance and are therefore not tied to any targets.

4. The bad practices that can hinder the success of the suggestion system include:

✓ Implementing a suggestion system in isolation without the support of the middle management

✓ Absence of participative management style, and organization structures are very rigid

✓ Paying least attention to suggestion implementation

✓ Suggestions are sought, but no rewards are given for employees' contributions.

✓ Restricting the participation to certain categories of employees only

✓ Making employees responsible for the effectiveness of the idea

# CHAPTER 4

# Is Your Idea Management System Sustainable? A Tool Kit

This chapter introduces a structured tool that can be applied to assess the sustainability of a suggestion system. The tool has been proposed based on the research that was carried out to understand the suggestion scheme characteristics and functionalities in different organizations using the suggestion schemes based in the United Arab Emirates.

The tool is structured around the five building blocks that we discussed in the previous chapter, and it allows companies to measure their scheme performance in great detail. It is hard to expect that each organization should perform consistently across each building block or indicator. It has been revealed that different practices are associated with each building block, and it requires different support activities to foster them. Organizations thus require addressing their particular strengths and weaknesses with regard to each indicator to equip themselves for the sustainability of their suggestion systems. So the tool helps to analyze each of the building blocks with the data that is uniquely useful for each organization. Through this assessment, organizations can develop distinctive approaches to sustain and yield desired results.

Building Block 1: Leadership and Top Management Support

**How and what practices demonstrate leadership and top management support of the suggestion scheme?**

Leadership and top management support is to be analyzed through four indicators: top management support, supervisor support, organizational support, and communication.

Top management support is usually exhibited through daily actions in a range of ways. These include formulating a vision and mission for a suggestion system. They also form strategies and procedures in support of the suggestion system and engage in awarding the employees. Supervisors encourage and guide their subordinates in making the suggestions. An organization facilitates its employees in taking part in the suggestion system by organizing creativity-related workshops, establishing nonrigid structures, and creating a supportive organization culture. Communication refers to the mechanism that the organization has in place to support the suggestion system. Organizations facilitate formal meetings among employees and create networking opportunities, such as participation in conferences or creativity-related activities. They may also establish an in-house newsletter and website to communicate and share information. Support for innovation implies how an organization can protect it employees from disputes as a result of suggestions from their coworkers. Organizations establish supportive HR polices and direct the suggestions to the supervisors for their initial evaluations. They empower supervisors to make decisions and also establish a central suggestion evaluation team. Coworkers help nurture the initial idea or help in formulating joint suggestions. They may collaborate to find solutions to issues and even provide support to promote colleagues' recommendations.

Building Block 2: System Capability

**What are features of the suggestion system?**

This block is be analyzed through five variables: rewards, feedback, evaluation, resources, and support for implementation.

Organizations require a mechanism to elicit employees' creative ideas, and therefore they must either have suggestion box, a manual system, or an automated system to elicit the ideas. This system should be monitored regularly, and the suggestions must be processed as per the organization's set policies and procedures. It is not sufficient to only receive the ideas and just appreciate them; they need to be implemented in full spirit in order for the organization to benefit from them. Organizations keep records of the suggestions received from their employees and the number of suggestions implemented after the evaluation of each of them. The success stories of this implementation must be published and made available for other employees to be motivated to make suggestions. Organizations hold promotional campaigns and make use of their bulletin boards, websites, and newsletters. They hold induction programs as well. Organizations usually have polices to process the suggestions within a stipulated date and provide feedback to the employer. Recognition may be handled through a well-defined reward scheme to include tangible or intangible benefits. Organizations have evaluation teams to assess the suggestions from employees. They have established evaluation procedures and rules on evaluation processes. The process of evaluation is made transparent to all employees. Resources and the allocation of a budget to award the suggestions are procedures for implementing a suggestion. Organizations set aside the financial budgets and establish procedures for employees to revert to if any physical resources are needed to facilitate the suggestion making or implementations.

Building Block 3: System Effectiveness

**What are the outcomes of the suggestion system, and how are these outcomes evidenced in the organization?**

This block is to be analyzed through four indicators: profitability, employee productivity, process improvement, and customer satisfaction.

Organizations can save cost or generate new revenues as a result of implemented suggestions. This can result in direct profit for the organization, or it can have indirect benefits such as:

- Improvement in employees' perceptions with regard to job satisfaction, sense of security, employee confidence, organizational commitment, and accountability
- Revisions to the processes and enhancement in product or service quality
- Customers satisfaction is improved.

Building Block 4: Organizational Encouragement

## What are the organizational mechanisms to support the suggestion schemes?

This block is to be analyzed through four indicators: teamwork, participation, training, and expertise.

Organizations realize the benefit of teamwork and encourage employees to collaborate and make joint suggestions. The awards would be designed to recognize the entire team. Employees can team up with colleagues from other departments as well. Employees are then subjected to creativity-related or system-related training to enhance their participation. They also organize events and workshops to stimulate creativity. Organizations make their suggestion system open to all employees and keep a record of suggestions received annually.

Building Block 5: System Barriers

## How well are organizational impediments addressed?

This factor is to be analyzed through two indicators: job control and competition.

Tight schedules, rigid job roles, and work pressures kill employee creativity. Organizations that don't give employees opportunities to think outside of the box and stick to exercising tasks or routines hinder creativity. At the same time, creating an atmosphere of completion among employees to test their abilities hinders the suggestion scheme process. The idea should be to make participation optional and at their will.

## Using the Tool to Assess the Suggestion Scheme's Effectiveness for Sustainability

This tool first helps to analyze which of the building blocks are at the initial, developmental, or advanced stage. The following survey tool should be completed table by table, as shown below. There are two primary ways to take this survey. Every individual in the organization can complete the survey and average the score, or the system administrator can complete the survey.

Example: The top management of this organization is proud that its system has become a benchmark for many other organizations in the United Arab Emirates, and they have affirmed a vision and a mission for their system. It recognizes its employees and supports annual conferences. The supervisor is at the heart of their system. It has an open communication format and networking opportunities to share and mingle with colleagues as required, and the organization arranges creativity workshops to stimulate creativity among its employees. Moreover, the high-value suggestions are seen as a result of cooperation and collaboration among colleagues. In this organization, supervisors are given an assurance that no suggestion would threaten their job roles, and at the same time the employees can make their suggestions to their supervisors; if these are not implemented, employees can propose the suggestion to a higher authority or to the central system.

Table to analyze Block 1

**Table 1: Block 1 Survey**

| Top Management Support | Characteristics | Scores |
|---|---|---|
| | No visible involvement of the top management in suggestion system | 1 |
| | Has established vision and mission for the system | 2 |
| | Has robust policies and procedures for the smooth functioning of the suggestion system | 2 |
| | Direct involvement of the top management for awarding the best suggestions | 3 |
| | Participation of the top management in the events relating to suggestion scheme | 3 |

| | | |
|---|---|---|
| | Top management is active in the review of the suggestion system performance monthly | 3 |
| | Hosting events and sponsoring events relating to creativity | 3 |
| | Giving strategic directives to improve performance | 3 |
| | Set up examples by involving themselves in making suggestions | 3 |
| Supervisor Support | Supervisors provide guidance and encouragement to submit ideas. | 1 |
| | Supervisor responsible for suggestion schemes as targets are set or are made accountable | 2 |
| | Opportunity to discuss work-related issues with supervisors prior to handing in a suggestion | 2 |
| | Supervisor provides guidance and assistance in refining the ideas and is empowered | 3 |
| | Supervisor and the line managers to the top are recognized for winning suggestions | 3 |
| | Supervisors review monthly or quarterly reports of the suggestion system performance. | 3 |
| Organizational Support | Clear suggestion guidelines and awareness to formulate suggestions | 1 |
| | No evidence or support to control disruptive behavior of coworkers | 1 |
| | Provision to dissolve any disputes among employees | 2 |
| | Supportive organizational culture | 2 |
| | Employees are given suggestion targets and are recognized during performance review. | 2 |
| | Hosts events to honor the winning suggestion | 2 |
| | Provision and good support to dissolve any disputes among employees | 3 |

| | Organization supports if an implemented suggestion needs to be replicated in other departments | 3 |
| --- | --- | --- |
| | Employees can also avail themselves of the support of the central suggestion scheme team should they need any help. | 3 |
| | Employee suggestions are centrally stored. | 3 |
| | Organizing creativity-stimulation workshops | 3 |
| Communication | Little evidence of open communication within the organization (e.g., formal or informal meetings) | 1 |
| | Minimum or no opportunity for networking internally and externally | 1 |
| | Good evidence of open communication within the organization | 2 |
| | Constant flow of information through websites, newsletters, etc. | 3 |
| | There are opportunities for networking internally and externally. | 3 |
| | Employees usually collaborate to make suggestions. | 2 |

**Table to analyze Block 2**

Example: This organization has a policy to consider a suggestion for awards only if it is implemented in the organization. It has a good record of suggestion implementations. Top management strongly believes in empowerment of employees and states that it is empowerment that has resulted in the success of the system. The technical expertise and experience of the employees have resulted in making award-winning suggestions at international levels. The suggestion tracking and feedback system of the organization is so encouraging that there is no rejection of a suggestion as such, but it is noted as "not being feasible to implement at this time" and stored on the database. The employees can monitor the progress of their suggestions online. The best part of their suggestion system is their awareness campaigns, which also won a prize at the international level. The system is simple to use, and, since its inception, it has gone through an evolution from a paper-based system to a highly sophisticated online system. The system, for example, is administered by the quality assurance department. Also, it has different categories of awards, such as best suggestion, best participation, CEO award, etc.

**Table 2: Block 2 Survey**

| Indicators | Characteristics | Scores |
|---|---|---|
| Rewards | There is a reward for the winning suggestion. | 1 |
| | Appreciation or award for taking part in local, regional, and international suggestion contests | 1 |
| | Financial and other types of rewards are set up, and the reward scheme is transparent. | 2 |
| | Rewards are fairly calculated as per the suggestions' savings. | 3 |
| | Established special annual award categories | 3 |
| Support of Implementation | Organizations usually implement suggestions. | 1 |
| | There is an improvement in the rate of suggestion implementations. | 2 |
| | Provision to replicate and implement solution elsewhere in the organization | 2 |
| | Awarding only implemented suggestions | 3 |
| | Monitoring the system performance with regard to suggestion implementation | 3 |
| | Employees are empowered to test their creativity. | 3 |
| Feedback | Set up reminders to evaluators and implementers on pending suggestions | 1 |
| | Set up realistic deadlines for processing the suggestions | 1 |
| | Provide encouraging feedback | 2 |

| | Provision to submit the suggestion to central administrator if needed | 3 |
|---|---|---|
| Evaluation | Dedicated schedule to evaluate the suggestions | 1 |
| | Dedicated evaluation team | 1 |
| | Evaluation criteria | 1 |
| | The evaluation procedures and team members are transparent. | 2 |
| | A chance to appeal the decision at least once | 3 |
| | Providing reasons for rejected suggestions | 3 |
| System Features | Multiple mechanisms to submit suggestions | 1 |
| | A user-friendly electronic system to receive and timely process the suggestion | 2 |
| | A user-friendly electronic system and dedicated suggestion scheme administrator | 3 |
| | Established roles and responsibilities for all stakeholders with regard to suggestion system | 3 |
| Awareness | There are some promotional campaigns and notification about the scheme. | 1 |
| | There are frequent promotional campaigns. | 2 |
| | The scheme has a brand name. | 3 |
| Resources | Availability of financial resources is limited. | 1 |
| | Adequate availability of financial resources and procedure to avail physical resources | 2 |
| | Additional management support to secure resources as required | 3 |

Table to analyze Block 3

Example: An organization demonstrates that it has achieved audited, cumulative savings amounting to $31.85 million from a total of 137,543 implemented and awarded suggestions. During 2011 alone, the company implemented more than twenty thousand suggestions, resulting in audited savings worth almost $4.36 million and 100 percent participation from eligible employees. It notes that the employees' creativity has resulted in enhancing the processes significantly and in improving their product quality. Over the course of their tenure, its production capacity has expanded tremendously.

**Table 3: Block 3 Survey**

| Indicator | Characteristics | Score |
|---|---|---|
| Profitability | There is no evidence of new revenue generation or cost savings. | 1 |
| | There is adequate evidence of new revenue generation or cost savings. | 2 |
| | There is good evidence of new revenue generation or cost savings. | 3 |
| Productivity | Employees are not satisfied, confident, and lack accountability. | 1 |
| | Employees are generally satisfied, confident, and show sense of responsibility. | 2 |
| | Employees are mostly satisfied, confident, accountable, and take responsibility. | 3 |
| Process Improvements | No process improvements taking place and no impact on products or services quality | 1 |
| | Some evidence of process improvements visible in product/service quality | 2 |
| | This is regular activity in the organization visible in product/service quality. | 3 |
| Customer Satisfaction | No evidence of improvement in customer satisfaction | 1 |
| | Adequate evidence of improvement in customer satisfaction | 2 |
| | Good evidence of improvement in customer satisfaction | 3 |

Table to analyze Block 4

Example: This organization recognizes the importance of teamwork and facilitates team suggestions. It is also noted that high-value suggestions are mostly team-based suggestions. Organization A also provides training to its employees to use the suggestion system and organizes creativity-related workshops; on average, each employee underwent 4.2 days of training. All employees are eligible to participate in the suggestion system, and it was noted that for the sixth consecutive year it received 100-percent participation from its employees. Top management repeatedly noted that the success of the suggestion system is purely due to the involvement of its employees.

### Table 4: Block 4 Survey

| Indicator | Characteristics | Score |
|-----------|-----------------|-------|
| Employee Participation | Participation in suggestion scheme is limited to few employees. | 1 |
| | Number of suggestions received are not known or made public. | 1 |
| | Scheme open to all to participate | 2 |
| | Evidence available to demonstrate the actual participation (number of suggestions) | 2 |
| | Organization has few talented employees. | 2 |
| | Organization or employees win awards for their suggestions | 3 |
| | High-value suggestions are elicited from experienced employees. | 3 |
| | Sets participation targets (minimum suggestions per year) | 3 |
| | Encourages suggestions for any area and not necessarily for cost savings | 3 |

| Teamwork | No provision for team suggestions | 1 |
|---|---|---|
| | Team suggestions are encouraged. | 2 |
| | Team rewards are established. | 3 |
| | Teams make high-value suggestions. | 3 |
| Training | No formal training is offered. | 1 |
| | Training programs are offered to use suggestion system. | 2 |
| | Creativity-related workshops and training are regular. | 2 |

Table to analyze Block 5

Example: Employees are given job autonomy for the fact that if employees' suggestions do not carry solutions, they will not be considered as valid suggestions. Moreover, the success of the suggestion system is attributed to empowerment, and no task reutilization or standard practices are to be followed strictly. The free flow of communication and creativity-related workshops mainly demonstrates a supportive culture within the organization rather than a controlling environment. Employees are expected to participate in the system at their will, and participation is not mandatory.

**Table 5: Block 5 Survey**

| Indicator | Characteristics | Score |
|---|---|---|
| Job Control | Little flexibility in working environment | 1 |
| | Usually standard work routines and mostly work under pressure | 1 |
| | Employees feel pressured to make suggestions as they believe they are judged for their performance through the suggestion system | 1 |
| | Usually no standard work routines and work under pressure | 2 |

| | Moderate flexibility in working environment | 2 |
|---|---|---|
| | Employees are somewhat informed that participation is not mandatory, but they are tied indirectly to its success through different target setting. | 2 |
| | Employees are well informed that they participate in suggestion scheme at their own will, and they are not judged for their performance and therefore are not tied to any targets. | 3 |
| | Good flexibility in working environment | 3 |
| | No standard work routines or work pressures | 3 |

The next step is to compare the evaluations to the below criteria:

**Table 6: Evaluation Criteria**

| Block 1 | Block 2 | Block 3 | Block 4 | Block 5 | **Overall** | **Result** |
|---|---|---|---|---|---|---|
| 1-6 | 1-11 | 1-4 | 1-4 | 1-3 | **<27** | **Initial Stage** |
| 7-20 | 12-6 | 5-8 | 5-12 | 4-6 | **28-62** | **Developmental Stage** |
| 21 and above | 16 and above | 9 and above | 12 and above | 6 and above | **63** | **Advanced Stage** |

Using this tool, organizations can pinpoint the indicators required for fostering its maximum benefits. The task is to then identify each of the blocks and their indicators that exhibit weakness and to develop potential strategies to foster the respective indicator.

### Moving Forward

The initial stage indicates that the organization has minimum requirements in place with respect to their suggestion scheme; as such, it requires nurturing and adopting the practices associated with the developmental stage. The developmental stage indicates a moderate existence of required support elements, but each of these indicators can be fostered further to achieve a higher level of performance by adopting the advanced level practices explained in chapter 3.

# CONCLUSION

A way forward is to focus on prioritizing problems identified by frontline employees who have real value.

Idea management systems have evolved from basic suggestion boxes to computer-based systems. As technology advances, it can be great tool for organizations to engage in employee involvement. The twenty-first-century workforce is likely to be more techno savvy, and tools such as these would be beneficial for employee engagement. The soft factors such as teamwork, collaboration, and networking can be greatly facilitated with more modern tools, and it would then be interesting to study if such mechanisms can have an impact on the performance of this tool. The virtual environments and flat organizations can break much of the barriers as well and give rise to a spurt of creativity. The twenty-first century calls for greater creativity and innovative skills.

The twenty-first-century workforce can thus put organizations in the learning mode. Learning organizations are still evolving. Capturing experiences and sharing them across the organization is becoming essential for survival.

So one way to look at this tool is as a vehicle that can guide organizations down the path to becoming learning organizations.

It is well acknowledged that creativity is one of the key pillars of success in a very competitive business world. So what is your organization doing about it?

**

# REFERECES

1. Chaneski, W. (2006), "The Suggestion Box Syndrome (And A Better Alternative)". Retrieved from http://www.mmsonline.com/columns.
2. Milner, E., Kinnell, M. & Usherwood, B. (1995), "Employee suggestion schemes: a management tool for the 1990s?", *Library Management*, Vol.16, No. 3, pp.3-8.
3. Arthur, J.B., Aiman-smith, L. and Arthur, J.E.F.B. (2010), "Gainsharing and organizational learning: suggestions over time an analysis of employee", *Management*, Vol.44, No.4, pp.737-754
4. Fairbank, J.F., Spangler, W., and Williams, S.D. (2003), "Motivating creativity through a computer-mediated employee suggestion management system", *Behaviour & Information Technology*, Vol. 22, No. 5, pp.305-314.
5. Du Plessis, A.J., Marx, A.E. and Wilson, G. (2008), "Generating ideas and managing suggestion systems in organisations: some empirical evidence", *International Journal of Knowledge, Culture and Change Management*, Vol. 8, No. 4, pp.133-140.
6. Arif, M., Aburas, H.M., Al Kuwaiti, A. and Kulonda, D. (2010)," Suggestion Systems: A Usability-Based Evaluation Methodology", *Journal of King Abdulaziz University-Engineering Sciences*, Vol. 21, No. 2, pp.61-79.
7. Islam, R. & Ismail, A.Z.H. (2008). "Employee motivation: a Malaysian perspective", International Journal of Commerce and Management, Vol.18, No.4, pp.344-362.
8. Carrier, C. (1998), "Employee Creativity and suggestion systems programs: An Empirical study", *Creativity and Innovation Management*, Vol. 7, No. 2, pp 62-72.
9. Lloyd., G.C. (1999), "Stuff the suggestion box", *Total Quality Management*, Vol, 10, No 6, pp.869-875

10. Harvey, D., (1973), "Ideas schemes: a new boost for profits?" Industrial *Management & Data Systems*, Vol.73, No.10, pp.26-30.

11. Ohly, S., Sonnentag, S. and Pluntke, F. (2006), "Routinization, work characteristics and their relationships with creative and proactive behaviors", *Journal of Organizational Behavior*, Vol.27, No.3, pp. 257-279.

12. Van Dijk, C. & Van den Ende, J. (2002), "Suggestion system: transferring employee creativity into practicable ideas", *R&D Management*, Vol. 32, No. 5, pp. 387-395.

13. Crail, M. (2006), "Fresh ideas from the floor", *Personnel Today*, pp.30.

14. Arthur, J.B., Aiman-smith, L. and Arthur, J.E.F.B. (2010), "Gainsharing and organizational learning: suggestions over time an analysis of employee", *Management*, Vol.44, No.4, pp.737-754

15. Fuller, U., Helbling, C., & Cooley, R. (2002), "Suggestion schemes as information and knowledge management system". In B. Howell & G. Orange (Eds.), "Information Systems Research, Teaching and Practice" Proceedings of the 7th Annual UKAIS Conference, Leeds Metropolitan University, England, UK (pp. 226-234). Leeds, UK: Leeds Metropolitan University.

16. Glover, W.J., Farris, J.A., Aken, E.M.V., & Doolen, T.L. (2011), "Critical success factors for the sustainability of Kaizen event human resource outcomes: An empirical study", *International Journal of Production Economics*, Vol.132, No.2, pp.197-213.

17. Basadur, M. (1992), "Managing creativity: a Japanese model", *Management*, Vol 6., No. 2, p. 25.

18. Chen, M.H. & Kaufmann, G. (2008), Employee Creativity and R&D: A Critical Review, *Creativity and Innovation Management*, Vol.17, No.1, pp.71-76.

19. Oldham, G.R. & Cummings, A. (1996), "Employee Creativity: Personal and Contextual Factors at Work", *Academy of Management Journal*, Vol.39, No.3, pp.607-634.

20. Baccarani, C. (2009), "What do you think creativity is and where can you find it?", *The Asian Journal of Quality*, Vol. 6, No. 22, pp. 91-101.

21. McAdam, R. & McClelland, J. (2002), "Individual and team-based idea generation within innovation management:

organizational and research agendas", *European Journal of Innovation Management*, Vol.5, No.2, pp.86-97

22. Rindasu, V.C. & Mihajlovic, I. (2008), "Idea Management for Organisational Innovation", Vol 15, No. 1, ISSN 1453-7397, pp.398-404.

23. Watson, E. (2007), "Who or What Creates? A Conceptual Framework for Social Creativity", *Human Resource Development Review*, Vol.6, No.4, pp.419-441.

24. Lam, A. (2010), "Organizational innovation to improve the efficiency of health care markets", *National Bureau of Economic Research bulletin on aging and health*, Vol.2, pp.1-2.

25. McLean, L.D. (2005). "Organizational Culture's Influence on Creativity and Innovation: A Review of the Literature and Implications for Human Resource Development", *Advances in Developing Human Resources*, Vol. 7 No. 2, pp. 226-246.

26. Khairuzzaman, W., Ismail, W. and Abdmajid, R. (2007), "Framework of the Culture of Innovation: A Revisit", *Jurnal Kemanusiaan*, Vol.9, pp. 38-49

27. Flynn, M., Dooley, L. & Cormican, K. (2003), "*Idea management for. International Journal of Innovation Management*, Vol. 7, No.4, pp.417-442.

28. Björklund and Magnusson, M. (2009), "Where Do Good Innovation Ideas Come From? Exploring the Influence of Network Connectivity on Innovation Idea Quality", *Journal of Product Innovation Management*, Vol.26, No. 6, pp. 662-670

29. Hoyrup, S. (2010), "Employee-driven innovation and workplace learning: basic concepts, approaches and themes", *Transfer: European Review of Labour and Research*, Vol.16 No.2, pp.143-154.

30. Leach, D.J., Stride, C.B. & Wood, S.J. (2006), "The effectiveness of idea capture schemes, *International Journal of Innovation Management*", Vol. 10, No. 3, pp.325-350

31. Tatter, M.A. (1975), "Tuning Ideas into Gold", *Management Review*, Vol.64, No.3, p.4.

32. Hayward, S. (2010), "Engaging employees through whole leadership", *Strategic HR Review*, Vol.9, No.3, pp.11-17.

33. Anderson, T.A. and Veillette, A. (2008)," Contextual Inhibitors of Employee Creativity in Organizations: The Insulating Role of

Creative Ability", *Group & Organization Management*, Vol.34, No.3, pp.330-357

34. Zhang, X., & Bartol, K. M. (2010), "Linking Empowering Leadership and Employee Creativity: the Influence of Psychological Empowerment, Intrinsic Motivation, and Creative Process Engagement", *Academy of Management Journal*, Vol. 53, No.1, pp.107-128.

35. Björklund, T. A. (2010), "Enhancing creative knowledge-work: challenges and points of leverage", *International Journal of Managing Projects in Business*, Vol.3, No.3, pp.517-525.

36. Malaviya, P., and Wadhwa, S. ( 2005), "Innovation Management in Organizational Context: An Empirical Study", *Global Journal of Flexible Systems Management*. Vol. 6, No. 2, pp. 1-14

37. Alwis, R.S. and Hartmann, E. (2008), "The use of tacit knowledge within innovative companies: knowledge management in innovative enterprises", *Journal of Knowledge Management*, Vol.12, No.1, pp.133-147.

38. Kesting, P. and Ulhoi, J.P. (2010), "Employee-driven innovation: extending the license to foster innovation", *Management Decision*, Vol.48, No.1, pp.65-84. 94.

39. Yuan, F. & Zhou, J. (2008), "Differential Effects of Expected External Evaluation on Different Parts of the Creative Idea Production Process and on Final Product Creativity", *Creativity Research Journal*, Vol.20 No.4, pp.391-403.

40. Madjar, N. (2008), "Emotional and informational support from different sources and employee creativity", *Journal of Occupational and Organizational Psychology*, Vol.81, No.1, pp.83-100.

41. Alves, J., Marques, M.J., Saur, I. & Marques, P. (2007), "Creativity and Innovation through Multidisciplinary and Multisectoral Cooperation", *Creativity and Innovation Management*, Vol.16, No.1, pp. 27-34

42. Koc, T. and Ceylan, C. (2007), "Factors impacting the innovative capacity in large-scale companies", *Technovation*, Vol 27, No. 3, pp.105-114

43. Attridge, M. (2009), "Measuring and Managing Employee Work Engagement: A Review of the Research and Business Literature", *Journal of Workplace Behavioral Health*, Vol.24, No.4, pp.383-398.

44. Mishra, J. M. (1994). "Employee Suggestion Programs in the Health Care Field: The Rewards of Involvement", *Public Personnel Management*, Vol. 23, No. 4, pp. 587

45. Sweins, C. & Jussila, I. (2010), "Employee knowledge and the effects of a deferred profit-sharing system: A longitudinal case study of personnel funds in Finland", *Thunderbird International Business Review*, Vol.52, No.3, pp.231-247

46. Ahmed, A. M. (2009), "Staff Suggestion Scheme (3Ss) within the UAE Context: Implementation and Critical Success Factors", *International Journal of Education, Business and Society: Contemporary Middle Eastern Issues*, Vol.2, No.2, pp.153-167

47. Crail, M. (2006), "Fresh ideas from the floor", *Personnel Today*, pp.30.

48. Stenmark, D. (2000), "Company-wide brainstorming: next generation suggestion systems?", Proceedings of IRIS 23, Laboratorium for Interaction Technology, University of Trollhättan Uddevalla, [online], available:www.viktoria.se/results/result_files/141.pdf

49. Rietzschel, E.F., Nijstad, B. A. & Stroebe, W. (2010), "The selection of creative ideas after individual idea generation: choosing between creativity and impact", British journal of psychology, Vol. 101, No. 1, pp.47-68.

50. Neagoe, L.N. and Klein, V.M. (2009). "Employee suggestion system ( kaizen teian ) the bottom-up approach for productivity improvement", *Control*, Vol.10, No. 3, pp.26-27

51. Tatter, M.A. (1975), "Tuning Ideas into Gold", *Management Review*, Vol.64, No.3, p.4.

52. Frese, M., Teng, E. and Wijnen, C.J.D. (1999), Helping to improve suggestion systems: predictors of making suggestions in companies", *Journal of Organizational Behavior*, Vol. 20, No.7, pp.1139-1155

53. Milner, E., Kinnell, M. & Usherwood, B. (1995), "Employee suggestion schemes: a management tool for the 1990s?", *Library Management*, Vol.16, No. 3, pp.3-8.

54. Westerveld, E. (2003), "The Project Excellence Modell: linking success criteria, and critical success factors", International Journal of Project Management, 21, 411-418

55. Gupta, A., McDaniel, J.C. & Herath, S.K. (2005.), "Quality management in service firms: sustaining structures of total quality service", *Managing Service Quality*, Vol.15, No.4, pp.389-402

56. McConville, J. (1990), "Innovation through involvement", The TQM Magazine, Vol. 2, No.5, pp.295-297.

57. Rapp, C. and Eklund, J. (2007), "Sustainable Development of a Suggestion System: Factors Influencing Improvement Activities in a Confectionary Company", *Human Factors*, Vol. 17, No.1, pp.79-94.

58. Baruah, J. & Paulus, P.B. (2008), "Effects of Training on Idea Generation in Groups", *Small Group Research*, Vol.39, No.5, pp.523-541

59. Madjar, N. (2005), "The Contributions of Different Groups of Individuals to Employees' Creativity", *Advances in Developing Human Resources*, Vol.7, No. 2. pp.182-206

60. Stranne.L. V. (1964), "Morale—The Key Factor In A Suggestion System", *Industrial Management*, Vol. 6, No. 11, pp.17

61. Axtell, C.M., Holman, D.J., Unsworth, K.L., WaU T.D. & Waterson, P.E. (2000), "Shop floor innovation: Facilitating the suggestion and implementation of ideas", *Journal of Occupational and Organizational Psychology*, Vol.73, No. 3, pp.265-285.

62. Wong, C.-keung S. & Pang, W.-L.L. (2003), "Barriers to creativity in the hotel industry—perspectives of managers and supervisors", *International Journal of Contemporary Hospitality Management*, Vol. 15, No. 1, pp.29-37

63. Sadi, M.A. and Al-Dubaisi, A.H. (2008)," Barriers to organizational creativity: The marketing executives' perspective in Saudi Arabia", *Journal of Management Development*, Vol. 27, No.6, pp.574-599.

64. Badiru, A.B. (2010), "Many Languages of Sustainability", *Industrial Engineer*, pp.30-35.

65. Garrido, P. (2009), "Business sustainability and collective intelligence", *The Learning Organization*, Vol.16, No.3, pp.208-222.

66. Aras, G. & Crowther, D. ( 2010), "Sustaining business excellence", *Total Quality Management & Business Excellence*, Vol.21, No.5, pp.565-576.

67. Zairi, M. &Liburd, I.M. (2001), "TQM sustainability—a roadmap for creating competitive advantage, Integrated Management, Proceedings of the 6th International conference on ISO 9000 and TQM, Paisley, Ayr, Scotland,17-19 April, pp.452-461. ISNB 963-86107-2-4

68. Jorgensen, T. H. (2008), "Towards more sustainable management systems: through life cycle management and integration, *Journal of Cleaner Production*, Vol.16, No.10, pp.1071-1080

69. Idris, M. & Zairi, M. (2006), "Sustaining TQM: A Synthesis of Literature and Proposed Research Framework", *Total Quality Management and Business Excellence*, Vol.17, No.9, pp.1245-1260

70. Bartel, C. & Garud, R. (2009), "The Role of Narratives in Sustaining Organizational Innovation", *Organization Science*, Vol.20, No.1, pp.107-117.

71. Ron, A.J.D., (1998). "Sustainable production : The ultimate result of a continuous improvement", *International Journal of Production Economics*, Vol.56, pp.99-110

72. Presley, A. & Meade, L. (2010), "Benchmarking for sustainability: an application to the sustainable construction industry", *Benchmarking: An International Journal*, Vol.17, No.3, pp.435-451

73. Labuschagne, C., Brent, A.C. & Erck, R.P.G. (2005), "Assessing the sustainability performances of industries", *Journal of Cleaner Production*, Vol.13, No. 4, pp.373-385.

74. Wood, N. & Contracts, B.M. (2005), "Making It Stick : Sustaining Your Improvements", *Control*, No.5, pp.24-26.

75. Svensson, G. (2006), "Sustainable quality management: a strategic perspective", *The TQM Magazine*, Vol.18, No.1, pp.22-29

# ABOUT THE AUTHOR

Dr Lasrado is an active researcher and specialist in the field of Kaizen and Employee suggestion scheme. Prior to this, she has published journal articles and presented papers at various conferences on ESS and Organizational Learning. She teaches Quality Management, Organizational Learning and Organizational Excellence modules at business schools. She is an ESS forum speaker and has conducted workshops and chaired panel discussions on suggestion schemes. Her expertise includes tailor made programs on suggestion scheme for organizations and conducting assessments for suggestion schemes. Visit www.flasrado.com for a detailed biography.